A Passion for Buttons!

More than 50 inspiring projects for chic and unique earrings, necklaces and rings

Stephanie Bourgeois

David and Charles

Project editor: Meriem Varone
Editorial co-ordinator: Valérie Gendreau
Editor: Martine Rousso
Proofreading: Sergine Greley and Édith Zha
Layout design: Susan Pak Poy
Layout: Frédérique Buisson
Illustrator: Lucie Niney
Photography: Francis Waldman
(cutout photos: Olivier Ploton)
Stylist: Véronique Méry
Cover: Agnès Frégé, Véronique Laporte
Mock-ups: Anne Raynaud
Photoengraving: Arts Graphiques du Centre

A DAVID & CHARLES BOOK
Copyright © Dessain et Tolra / Larousse 2006
Originally published in France as *Passionnément Bouton*
First published in the UK in 2007 by David & Charles

David & Charles is an F+W Publications Inc. company
4700 East Galbraith Road
Cincinnati, OH 45236

A catalogue record for this book is available from the British Library.

ISBN-13: 978-0-7153-2652-7 paperback
ISBN-10: 0-7153-2652-X paperback

Printed in China by Shenzhen Donnelley Printing Co Ltd
for David & Charles
Brunel House   Newton Abbot   Devon

Visit our website at www.davidandcharles.co.uk

David & Charles books are available from all good bookshops; alternatively you can contact
our Orderline on 0870 9908222 or write to us at FREEPOST EX2 110, D&C Direct,
Newton Abbot, TQ12 4ZZ (no stamp required UK only); US customers call 800-289-0963
and Canadian customers call 800-840-5220.

contents

basic equipment

BUTTONS

Whether second-, third- or fourth-hand or bought especially for the occasion, buttons come in all different shapes and sizes, with shanks or holes, and in a wide range of materials: mother-of-pearl, wood, plastic, metal, fabric, and many more.

You can even make your own buttons by covering them in the fabric of your choice (see page 52).

TOOLS

The designs in this book require a set of basic tools.

Scissors

1 **Pliers**
- Flat-nosed pliers often have a cutting edge and are used for crushing crimp beads, closing bead tips, crushing leather crimps and opening and closing jump rings.
- Round-nosed pliers are used mainly for making loops in the wire.
- Wire cutters are used to cut lengths of metal wire.

Slow-drying glue
This glue keeps its elasticity well and won't stand proud when it dries, unlike superglue.

1

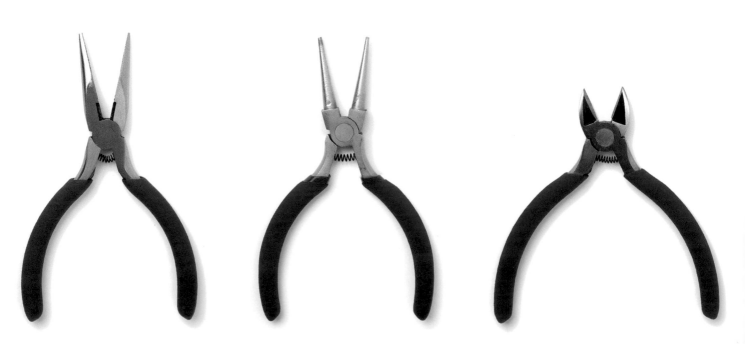

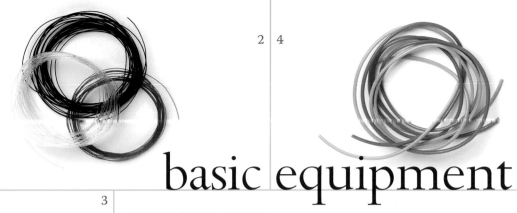

basic equipment

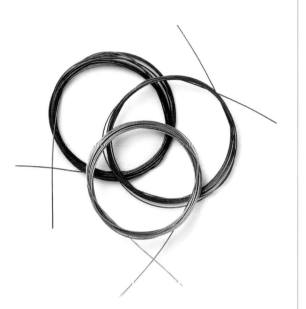

THREADS AND WIRES

2 **Nylon thread**
Nylon thread comes in a variety of colours and thicknesses. It is often secured to clasps using crimp beads because knots in nylon thread tend to unravel. It is mainly used in lightweight and flexible designs.

3 **Tiger tail**
Tiger tail is a metal wire coated in clear or coloured plastic. Secure using crimp beads. Tiger tail is a strong but delicate wire that marks when bent. It is particularly suited to heavier designs.

4 **Scoubidou strands**
These hollow plastic strands are easy to cut to size. To make them bendable, thread a length of stainless steel or brass wire into the centre of the strand.

5 **Coloured copper wire**
The copper wire is coated in coloured enamel. It is very easy to shape but is also very fragile and snaps if twisted repeatedly.

6 **Brass wire and stainless steel wire**
These two wires are much stronger than copper wire (stainless steel wire is very strong, but is harder to find). Use them to create more solid designs.

7 **Elasticated nylon thread**
This thick and soft thread is easy to knot. Use leather crimps to secure several strands on to one clasp.

8 **Leather thonging**

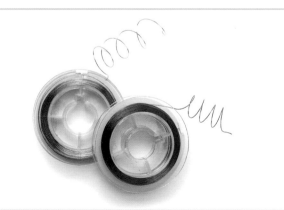

basic equipment

CLASPS

9 There are several different types of clasp: barrel clasps (avoid using these on heavy designs as they may come undone) and bolt rings and trigger clasps, which attach to double rings for greater stability (similar to keyrings).

In addition to these, some designs are more suited to a button and button loop system.

RINGS

10 **Jump rings**
These rings are broken and are used to join pieces together.

11 **Double rings**
Double rings are stronger than jump rings, are harder to open and are used mainly in conjunction with bolt rings and trigger clasps.

END PIECES

12 **Leather crimps**
These are used to attach lengths of leather thonging to clasps when they are too thick to be secured directly on to rings. To secure, place the thonging in the crimp with a little glue and close the crimp using flat-nosed pliers. Attach the crimps to the clasp with jump rings.

13 **Bead tips**
Use these to attach multiple strands to the same clasp. They can be closed around a knot or a crimp bead which secures all the wires or threads together. For added strength, apply a little glue to your knot or crimp bead before closing the bead tip.

14 **Crimp beads**
These are small metal beads that come in different sizes. Use them to secure nylon thread or tiger tail when knotting is impractical.

perfume…

Beware: costume jewellery is particularly susceptible to perfume damage. The alcohol and chemicals it contains can cause colour loss and damage your beads and buttons. Spray on perfume before putting on your jewellery and avoid areas in which it will be worn.

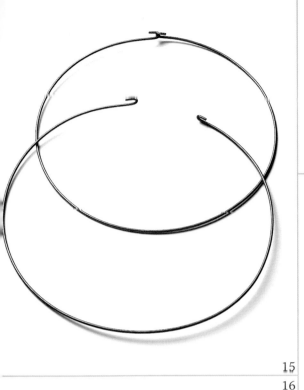

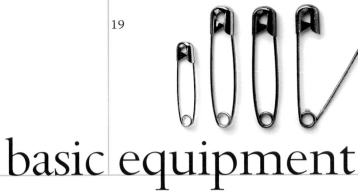

basic equipment

MOUNTS AND FINDINGS

15 **Chokers**
These come with hook clasps or screw fasteners.

16 **Ring blanks**
Flat mounts are used for designs that can be glued on. Mesh mounts come in two sections: a mesh part that you can work on and a base section that the mesh clips into when finished.

17 **Earrings**
• Glue designs on to flat earring findings.
• Hang drop earrings from fishhook earwires.

18 **Hairslide mounts**
If you can, use clips with a hole at each end, as this makes it easier to secure your creations.

19 **Safety pins**

15
16

17

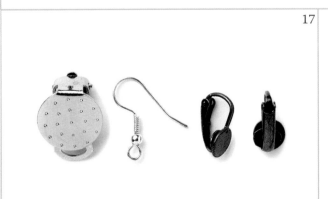

18

hints and tips

preparation
Create a mock-up of your design on a flat surface so you can see how it will look and make any changes before you start work.

symmetry
Always start at the centre of a piece and work outwards to keep the design symmetrical.

* Easy as ABC

Mother-of-pearl buttons threaded on to a length of cord.
You'll have this necklace and bracelet made in no time at all!

Materials required: necklace and bracelet

- Two-hole coloured mother-of-pearl buttons in different shapes and sizes
- Leather thonging or fine glacé cotton, about 50cm (20in) for the necklace and 20cm (8in) for the bracelet
- 2 leather crimps for each piece
- 2 jump rings for each piece
- 1 clasp for each piece

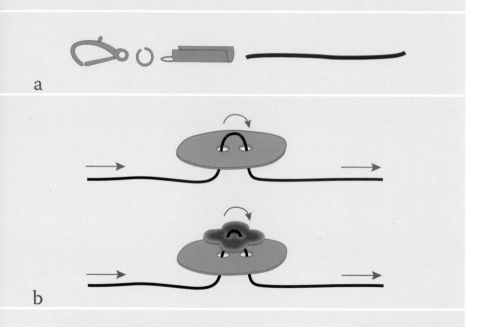

a

b

Materials required: hairslide

- 1 hairslide mount
- A few two-hole coloured mother-of-pearl buttons
- 20cm (8in) leather thonging or fine glacé cotton

Necklace and bracelet

Use the same technique for both pieces

1 Before starting, plan the position of the buttons (you could make your creations symmetrical, overlap your buttons, place small buttons on big ones or leave spaces between each button).

2 Secure one end of the leather thonging or glacé cotton in a crimp with a little glue. Close the crimp with flat-nosed pliers and attach it to the clasp using a jump ring. [▶a]

3 Thread the first button on to the cord from the back and go back through the second hole as if you were sewing on a button. Repeat until all your buttons are threaded on, spacing them out or overlapping them as desired. Try placing a small button on top of a larger one for a different effect. [▶b]

4 When you have gone as far as you need to go on your necklace or bracelet, secure the other end of the thonging in a leather crimp, attach the other jump ring and then the clasp.

Hairslide

Thread your buttons on to the thonging as shown in step 3 and thread the ends into the holes in the mount. Pull the cord tight and tie two tight knots. If necessary, apply a little glue to the underside of the overlapping buttons to keep them in place.

* Miscellany

This assortment of coloured buttons makes a fun piece.

Materials required: necklace and bracelet

- Assorted coloured buttons with holes or shanks
- Coloured nylon thread, about 1.2m (47in) per necklace row and 50cm (20in) per bracelet row
- 2 bead tips for each item
- 2 crimp beads for each item
- 2 jump rings for each item
- 1 clasp for each item

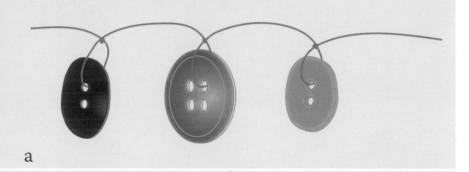

a

b

Materials required: rings and earrings

- 2 buttons of different sizes for each item
- 1 sequin
- 1 paste bead 4mm (⁵⁄₃₂in) in diameter
- Flat ring or earring mounts
- Glue

Necklace and bracelet

Use the same technique for both pieces

1 Sort out your buttons and make as many piles of buttons as you want rows. Thread the buttons on one at a time and tie a double knot with the ends of your thread after each button. Leave 3–4cm (1⅛–1½in) between each button, depending on their size. [▶a]

2 Repeat step 1 until you reach the desired length. Then make up each additional row in the same way. Make sure the colours and shapes of your buttons are evenly balanced.

3 Join the ends of the rows together using a crimp bead each end of your necklace (or bracelet), then close in a bead tip with a little glue. Attach the bead tips to the clasp using jump rings if necessary. [▶b]

Rings and earrings

To make rings or earrings, simply glue the different parts together, working from the largest to the smallest pieces.

*** Pop art

These brightly coloured buttons look a little like sweets. Warning: do not eat!

Materials required: necklace and bracelet

- Assorted brightly coloured buttons with holes, 20–25 in a range of sizes for the necklace, about 12 same size buttons for the bracelet
- Coloured copper wire, necklace: 6 x 1.5m (58⅞in) for the base and about 4m (4⅜yd) for attaching the buttons bracelet: 6 x 70cm (27½in) for the base and about 2m (2⅛yd) for attaching the buttons

a

b

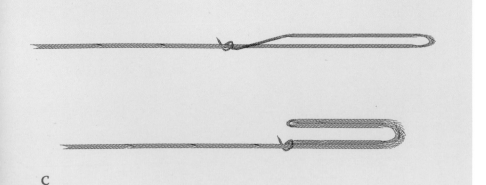

c

To make the base structure

1 Carefully fold the six lengths of wire in half. Using three wires, plait from each side of the centre of these six wires for 3cm (1⅛in), then twist the six ends of the plait together to make a button loop. [▶a]

2 Divide the 12 resulting lengths of wire into three groups and plait together for about 47cm (18½in). [▶b]

3 To make the clasp, bend the plait back on itself about 2.5cm (1in) from the end. Trim the remaining wires, leaving around 2cm (¾in) excess wire. Twist up this excess and crush with pliers around the plait. Bend the doubled plait in half to form a hook which will attach to the button loop. [▶c]

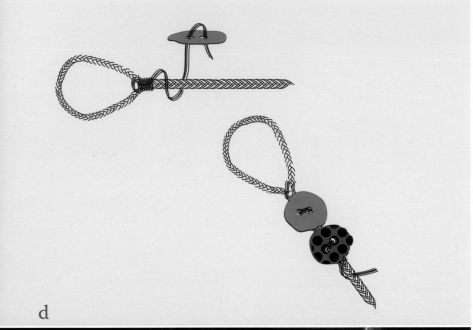

d

To attach the buttons

4 Lay your buttons out in order of size from the smallest to the largest and then the largest to the smallest so that the biggest buttons are at the centre of the necklace. Lay the necklace base out flat with the clasp undone.

5 Fold the 4m (4³⁄₈yd) length of copper wire in half. Thread this double wire into your button loop and double it again to give you four lengths of wire. Wind these four lengths once around the plait and thread on your first button from the underside. Go through the second hole in the button, as if you were sewing over the plait, and repeat with the next button, making sure you leave no space between them. Keep your wires tight so the buttons sit flat on top of the plait. [▶d]

6 When you have gone all the way around the necklace, turn your work over and use the remaining wire to tie a loop under each button to secure your work.

hints and tips

To make the bracelet, follow the same steps as for the necklace, working on a plait of about 20cm (8in).

Earrings

Materials required: earrings

- 2 pairs of buttons in different sizes and colours
- 2 fishhook earwires
- 50cm (20in) coloured copper wire

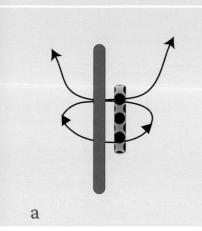

a

b

1 Place two buttons of different sizes one on top of the other. Fold a 25cm (9⅞in) length of wire in half and thread on the two buttons through one of the holes in the buttons, then cross the ends of wire in the second hole. [▶a]

2 Using round-nosed pliers, make a loop with the four lengths of wire over the top of the buttons. Attach this to the earwire. [▶b]

✶✶ Black & white

This necklace and matching bracelet have
a striking checkerboard effect.

Materials required: necklace

- 10 black and white two-hole buttons and a slightly
  larger button for the bottom of the necklace
- 5m (5½yd) stainless steel or brass wire, 0.4mm or
  0.5mm (0.015–0.022in) in diameter
- Choker in the same colour as the wire

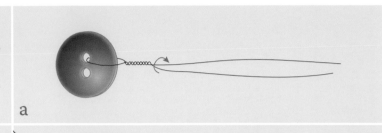

a

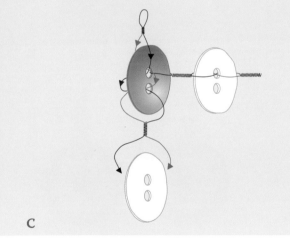

b

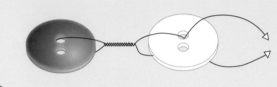

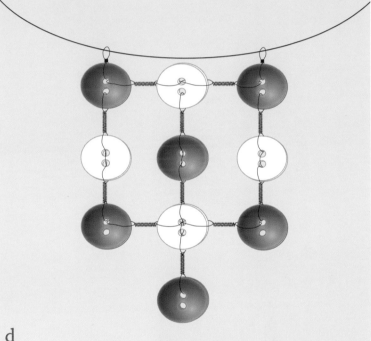

c

d

Alternate the colours of your buttons for a checkerboard effect

1 Thread a 1m (39¼in) length of wire into one of the holes
in the first button, double it at the centre and twist it for
2cm (¾in). [▶a]

2 Cross the two resulting wires in one of the holes of the
second button, twist the wires for another 2cm (¾in) and
attach the last button in the row, twisting and crushing
the excess wire behind that button. Make up another row
of three buttons using the same technique. [▶b]

3 Take 1m (39¼in) wire, double it and twist it around itself to
form a small loop (which will go round the choker). Next,
cross the wires through both holes in the first button in the
first row, twist the wire for 2cm (¾in), thread on a button in
the other colour, twist for another 2cm (¾in) and attach to
the first button in the last row. [▶c]

4 Repeat for the third column, then for the centre column,
without making a loop at the top this time but instead
attaching the larger button at the bottom of the
necklace. Twist the ends of wire behind the buttons and
apply a little glue. Turn the loops sideways and thread on
to the choker. [▶d]

Bracelet

Materials required: bracelet

- 12 black and white buttons and 1 for the clasp
- 3m (3¼yd) stainless steel or brass wire 0.5mm (0.022in) diameter

1 Attach the 12 buttons in pairs in the same way as for the necklace.

2 Cut a 1.5m (58⅞in) length of wire. Fold in half to work with it double. Make a button loop at its centre by bending the wire and twisting it. The loop should fit over the size of the button you are keeping for the clasp. [▶a]

3 Assemble the different parts in the same way as for the necklace, ending with the clasp button. [▶b]

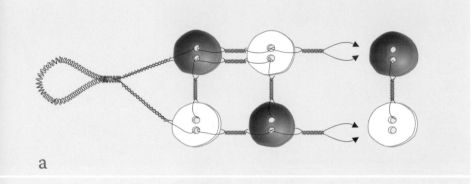

a

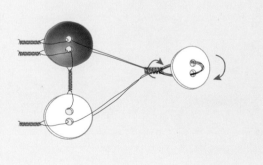

b

Earrings and pendant

Materials required: earrings

- 4 black and white buttons, 2 small, 2 large
- 60cm (23½in) silver wire
- 2 fishhook earwires

Materials required: pendant

- 1 large, 1 medium black and white button and 4 small black buttons
- 1 choker
- Stainless steel wire 0.5mm (0.022in) in diameter and 5 times the circumference of the choker

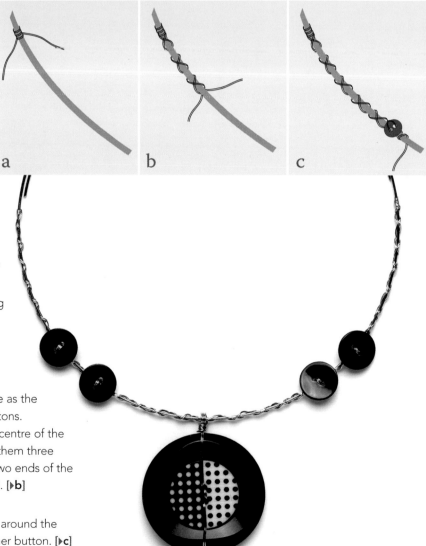

a

b

c

Earrings

Work in the same way as for the necklace and bracelet, twisting the wire between each pair of buttons. Make a small ring at the top of the design using round-nosed pliers. Attach the ring to the earwire.

Pendant

1 Make up the pendant using the same technique as the earrings, twisting the wire between the two buttons.
   Fold the length of wire in half and attach the centre of the two wires at one end of the choker by winding them three times around the structure [▶a], then wind the two ends of the wire in opposite directions for about 4cm (1½in). [▶b]

2 Thread on the first black button, wind the wires around the choker for a short distance and thread on another button. [▶c]
   Continue twisting the wire to the centre of the choker.

3 Thread on the pendant and finish the second side to match the first. Wind the wires round the end to fix and secure with a little glue.

✳✳ Satin sheen

This chic bronze and satin set is easy to assemble.

Materials required: necklace

- 15–20 assorted natural or bronze mother-of-pearl buttons with holes, in different shapes and sizes
- 4m (4³⁄₈yd) fine stainless steel or brass wire
- 1.5m (58⁷⁄₈in) narrow ecru satin ribbon

a

b

Materials required: earrings

- 4 bronze buttons, 2 x 22mm (⁷⁄₈in) in diameter, 2 x 18mm (¹¹⁄₁₆in) in diameter
- 2 smaller mother-of-pearl leaf-shaped buttons
- 2 natural buttons, 12mm (½in) in diameter
- 2 fishhook earwires
- 2 x 25cm (9⁷⁄₈in) stainless steel or brass wire

c

If you are looking to create a specific shape, lay your buttons out before threading them on. If not, start from scratch and let inspiration be your guide!

Necklace

1 Cut the wire in half and work with both wires at the same time. Double up the wires and use round-nosed pliers to twist them to make a small loop at one end of the work. This will be used to attach the ribbon.

2 Thread on the first button, crossing the pairs of wire through the holes and bring them out together to twist at the top of the button. [▶a]

3 Work either side of the first button using the same technique. Twist the wire gently between each button. [▶b]

4 Link all the buttons together, as randomly as possible. You can create links between buttons, overlap some of them and place small buttons over larger ones.

5 Finish off with a single button and then make a second loop as in step 1. Cut the ribbon in two and attach one length to each loop. Tie the necklace around your neck or attach a clasp using leather crimps.

Earrings

Thread a large button and a leaf-shaped button in the centre of the wire. Cross the wires through the second hole of the buttons and twist them by making three turns over the top. Next, thread on the medium-sized bronze button with the small natural button on top. Make a loop at the top of the motif using round-nosed pliers. Attach to a fishhook earwire using a jump ring if necessary. [▶c]

✳ Ethnic chic

Wood and mother-of-pearl make perfect partners
in this ethnic-inspired jewellery.

Materials required: necklace

- 15 two-hole buttons, 3–4cm (1⅛–1½in) in
  diameter, in a range of natural materials
- 3m (3¼yd) stainless steel or brass wire, 0.5mm
  (0.022in) in diameter

a

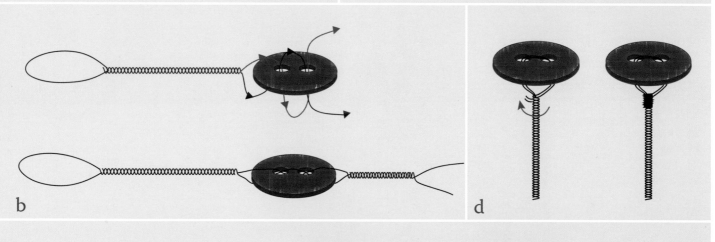

b

d

c

1 Make a button loop at one end of the necklace by
doubling your wire and twisting it back around itself. Bear
in mind the size of the button that will be placed at the
other end of your necklace as the clasp. [▶a]

2 Twist the wire for about 5cm (2in), then thread on the first
button, crossing the wires over in the holes. [▶b]

3 Repeat this step, spacing out the buttons at random
intervals of twisted wire and varying the button materials
as you go. [▶c]

4 When you have reached your desired length, attach the
clasp button by threading the two wires into the same
button hole towards the front, then go back through
the button via the other hole and wind the excess wire
around the twisted base. [▶d]

Materials required

- 1 wooden chopstick

To make the straight hairstick:

- 3 assorted two-hole buttons in natural materials
- 1.5m (58⅞in) stainless steel or brass wire, 0.4mm (0.015in) in diameter

To make the fan hairstick:

- 4–6 assorted two-hole buttons in natural materials
- 1.5m (58⅞in) stainless steel or brass wire, 0.4mm (0.015in) in diameter

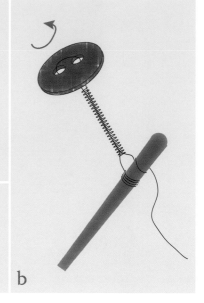

b

a

Straight hairstick

1 Plan the order in which you will thread on your buttons and start by threading on the button that will sit at the top of the stick in the middle of the wire. Turn the button around on itself to twist the wire for 3cm (1⅛in).

2 Cross the wires in the second button, then twist the wire again, this time for 2cm (¾in). Next, go through the last button, then wind the wires around the thickest part of the chopstick. Hide the ends under the last button. [▶a]

Fan hairstick

1 Wind one end of the wire three times around the stick 3cm (1⅛in) from the top, then thread on a button 4cm (1½in) from the stick. Turn it around on itself to twist the wire and then wind it round the stick again. [▶b]

2 Repeat this step, attaching your buttons at different heights. When you have finished, hide the end of the wire under your last button, adding a little glue to hold. Bend the strands using a pair of pliers to create angles.

Earrings

Materials required

- 1 or 2 two-hole buttons per earring
- 2 x 15cm (5⅝in) brass or stainless steel wire
- 2 fishhook earwires

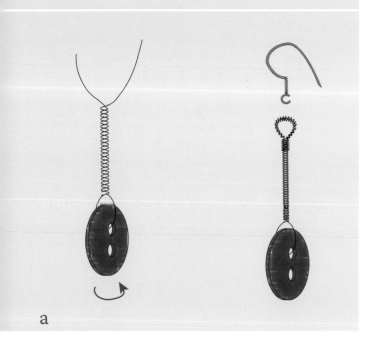

a

Single-button earrings

1 Thread a button into the centre of the wire and bend the wire back on itself. Turn the button around to twist the wire for about 3cm (1⅛in).

2 Using round-nosed pliers, create a loop at the top of the wire. Attach this loop to your fishhook earwire. [▶a]

Two-button earrings

Use the same technique as for the single-button earrings, this time using a small and a large button, one on top of the other.

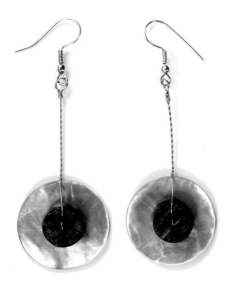

✳✳ Echoes of Africa

Safety pins are teamed up with metal, wood and beads in these exciting designs.

Materials required

- 13–15 assorted metal shank buttons
- Wooden beads
- About 80 safety pins
- 50cm (20in) length of tiger tail
- 2 crimp beads
- 1 clasp

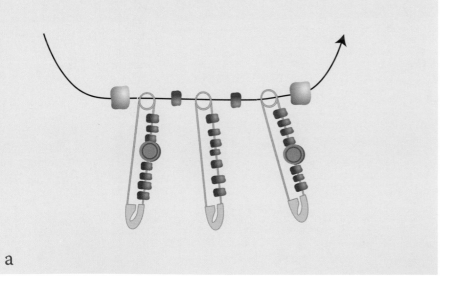

a

1 Thread your beads and buttons on to the safety pins.

2 Gently crush the clasps on the safety pins with flat-nosed pliers so they can no longer be undone.

3 Attach the clasp to the tiger tail with a crimp bead as follows: thread on a crimp bead, go through the ring in the clasp, go back through the crimp bead and flatten with flat-nosed pliers.

4 Thread on a wooden bead, then a safety pin, threading the tiger tail into the end ring, and repeat until you reach your desired length. Make sure you thread all the pins on in the same way and that they are only held at one end so as to fit round your neck. [▶a]

5 Attach the second half of the clasp as described in step 3.

hints and tips

If you are making a symmetrical necklace, start at the centre and work outwards.

Earrings and bracelet

Materials required: earrings

- 2 metal shank buttons
- 2 safety pins
- Wooden beads
- 1 pair fishhook earwires
- 2 jump rings

Materials required: bracelet

- 13–15 assorted metal shank buttons
- Wooden beads
- Metal faceted beads with large holes
- About 30 safety pins
- About 50cm (20in) round elastic

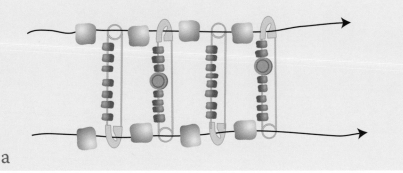

a

Earrings

1 Thread the beads and buttons on to the safety pins. Crush the clasps gently to prevent them opening.

2 Attach the pins to the earwire mounts using jump rings.

Bracelet

1 Thread the beads and buttons on to the safety pins, bearing in mind that the pins will be arranged head to tail.

2 Gently crush the clasps on the safety pins using flat-nosed pliers so they no longer open.

3 Cut the elastic in half. Thread on the safety pins head to tail, adding a metal bead between each pin. Work with both lengths of elastic at the same time, one strand going through the ring in the pin and the other through the clasp. Continue until you reach your desired length. [▶a]

4 To finish the bracelet, tie a knot to join the ends of the strands of elastic. Apply a little glue to the knot and hide it under a bead or pin.

✳ Chinoiserie

Ribbons and tassels complement large buttons in these gloriously oriental designs.

Materials required: necklace

- 2 large, dark coloured buttons, 1 x 6cm (2⅜in) in diameter, 1 x 3cm (1⅛in) in diameter
- 2 coloured tassels
- 2 x 1.5m (58⅞in) ribbon, one narrower than the other
- 2 x 25cm (9⅞in) narrow satin ribbon

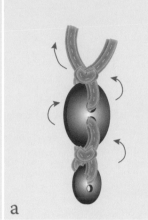

a

b

Materials required: brooch

- 3–4 braided ball buttons in different sizes and colours
- 2–3 two-hole buttons in different sizes and colours
- 1 kilt pin
- 2 x 15cm (5⁶⁄₈in) narrow coloured satin ribbons
- 40cm (15⅝in) coloured copper wire
- 3 jump rings

c

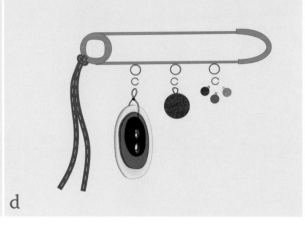

d

Necklace

1 Work with both the 1.5m (58⅞in) ribbons at the same time. Thread the small button into the centre of the ribbons and tie them in a knot over the top of the

2 Thread on the large button above the small button, crossing your ribbons in the button holes. Tie a knot in the ribbons above the second button. [▶a]

3 Attach the tassels and the narrow ribbon to the small button at the bottom. [▶b] Tie the ends of the ribbons round your neck or attach to a clasp.

Brooch

1 Fold the 40cm (15⅝in) length of copper wire in half and thread one or more buttons into the centre in order of size. Cross the wires in the second hole of the buttons and twist them together on top of the button. Make a loop using round-nosed pliers. [▶c]

2 Attach the flat buttons and ball-shaped buttons to the kilt pin with jump rings. Two or three small ball buttons can fit on one jump ring. Tie lengths of ribbon directly on to the pin and through the end ring. [▶d]

✳ Bright braided balls

These ribbon and braided button compositions make delicate pieces.

Materials required: pendant

- 7 small braided ball buttons in different colours
- 70cm (27½in) narrow satin ribbon

Materials required: earrings

- 8 small braided ball buttons in different colours
- 2 jump rings, about 8mm (5/16in) in diameter
- 2 fishhook earwires

a

b

Materials required: necklace

- 20–25 small braided ball buttons in different colours
- 80cm (31³/8in) thin cord
- 2 leather crimps
- 1 clasp
- 2 jump rings

c

d

Pendant

1 Thread the first button into the centre of the ribbon.

2 Thread all your remaining buttons on to both ends of the ribbon on top and each side of the first. [▶a]

3 Once you have threaded on all the buttons, tie a knot above them to keep them in place. Tie the necklace directly around your neck or attach a clasp using leather crimps.

Earrings

Open the jump rings and thread four small ball buttons on each one. Attach them on to the earwires, closing the jump rings. [▶b]

Necklace

1 Secure one end of the cord to a leather crimp with a small amount of glue and close to hold using a pair of flat-nosed pliers. [▶c]

2 Thread the ball buttons on to the cord, tying a knot after every three or four buttons to keep them in place. [▶d]

3 Once you have reached your desired length, attach the second crimp and then attach the clasp using jump rings.

✳✳ Sunshine

These sunny designs will brighten up any occasion!

Materials required: pendant

- 1 large two-hole button
- Assorted smaller beads and buttons in different colours
- 4m (4⅜yd) coloured copper wire
- 2 x 80cm (31⅜in) narrow satin ribbon in two colours

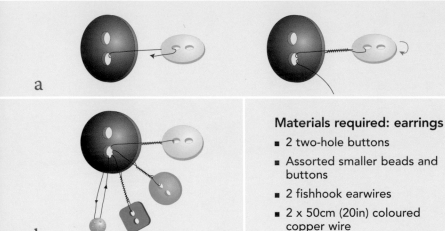

a

b

Materials required: earrings

- 2 two-hole buttons
- Assorted smaller beads and buttons
- 2 fishhook earwires
- 2 x 50cm (20in) coloured copper wire

Materials required: brooch

- 1 large two-hole button
- Assorted smaller beads and buttons
- 1 brooch mount
- 4m (4⅜yd) coloured copper wire

Pendant

1 Thread the copper wire into one of the holes in the large button, leaving 5cm (2in) excess to finish off your work. Thread on a bead or small button about 3cm (1⅛in) from your large button. Bend your wire back and turn the bead (or button) around on itself to twist the wire. [▶a]

2 Go back through the same hole in the large button in the opposite direction and repeat this step, spacing out the beads and buttons to radiate out from the centre in a semi-circle. [▶b]

3 Finish by taking the two ends of the copper wire through the top hole in opposite directions and over the top of the button. Bring the ends of wire together, twist them around and make a loop with round-nosed pliers. Flatten the ends behind the button, adding a little glue to secure. Thread your finished piece on to the ribbons and tie round your neck with a knot.

Earrings

Work in the same way as for the pendant, attaching the loops at the top to the earwires.

Brooch

Work in the same way as for the pendant this time making the beads radiate all round the button. Glue the brooch mount to the back of the large button. To secure your work to the mount and add a fun touch, knot a small length of ribbon in the centre of the button.

***Winter wonders

Easy-to-wear creations in similar shades of wool.

Materials required

- About 30 two- or four-hole buttons in different colours and sizes
- 1 ball multi-coloured wool for 4.5mm (UK/US 7) knitting needles
- 1 pair knitting needles 4.5mm (UK/US 7)
- 1 crewel needle

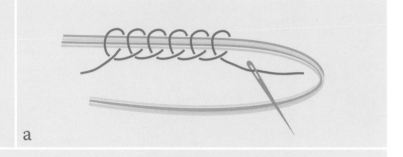

a

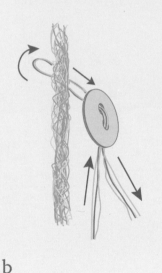

b

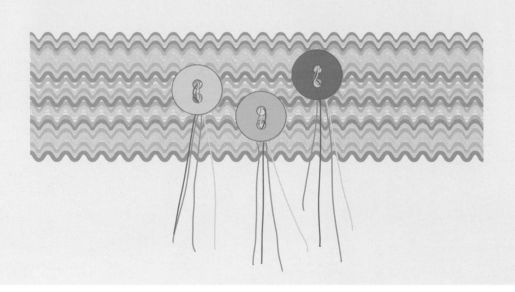

1   Cast on 10 stitches and knit a strip of garter stitch (knit stitch throughout) for the length of your necklace, about 35–40cm (13¾–15⅝in).

2   Sew on a button at one end of the strip for the clasp and create a button loop with buttonhole stitch worked over strands of wool at the other end. [▶a]

3   Thread a length of wool into the needle and work with it double. Thread on a button from underneath through both holes, stitch to a row of knitting and go back through the button in the opposite direction. Leave about 10cm (4in) wool ends and cut off the rest. Tie a knot to secure the button flat against the knitting. [▶b]

4   Repeat this step adding buttons and fringing until you have achieved your desired effect. You can add strands of wool without buttons, too.

* Pyramids

Stacked-up buttons add dramatic volume to this simple design.

Materials required: necklace

- Thick two-hole buttons in different sizes and colours
- 2 x 2m (2⅛yd) cord or narrow ribbon

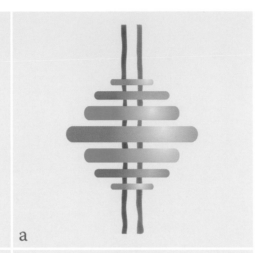

a

Materials required: earrings

- Thick two-hole buttons in different colours and sizes
- 4 crimp beads
- 1 pair fishhook earwires
- 2 x 15cm (5⅝in) tiger tail

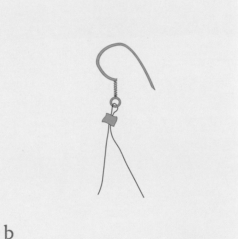

b

c

Necklace

1 Thread on the buttons from the smallest to the largest and then back to the smallest to form a double pyramid. Use two strands of cord or ribbon to go through the two button holes at the same time. Secure the buttons with a knot on either side. [▶a]

2 Repeat this process, spacing them at 5–10cm (2–4in) intervals and varying the number of buttons used.

3 When you have reached your desired length, tie a knot in the ends of the ribbons and either leave the excess hanging down or cut it off. Why not brighten up your design by using different coloured ribbons?

hints and tips

Make sure the weight of your necklace is well balanced. Work from the centre outwards to ensure your work is symmetrical.

Earrings

1 Fold the tiger tail in half and attach to the earwire using a crimp bead. [▶b] Thread on the button pyramid.

2 Secure the two ends of tiger tail below the buttons with a crimp bead. Trim off the excess. [▶c]

* Cascade

Nylon thread and mother-of-pearl add a refreshing touch to this necklace.

Materials required

- Assorted colours of two-hole mother-of-pearl buttons in different shapes and sizes
- Coloured nylon thread, about 1.2m (47in) per necklace row and 1.5m (58⅞in) per hanging section
- 2 bead tips
- 2 crimp beads
- 1 clasp

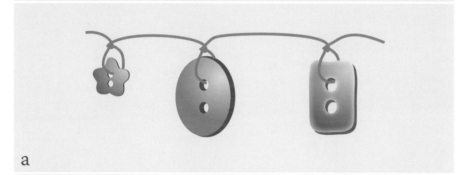

a

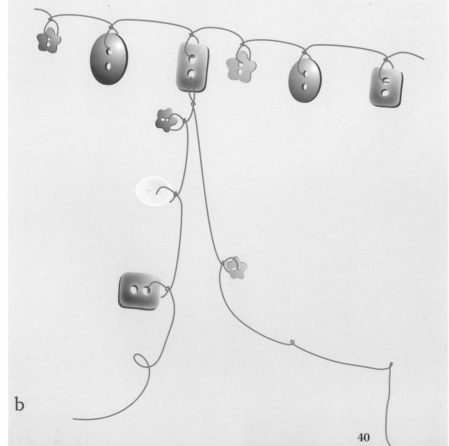

b

1 Set aside about 20 buttons for the hanging sections and divide up the remaining buttons according to how many rows you intend to create.

2 For the first row thread the buttons one by one on to the nylon thread tying a double knot over each one. Space the buttons at 3–4cm (1⅛–1½in) intervals depending on their size. Repeat until you have reached your desired length, spreading the colours and shapes out evenly. Make up the other rows using this technique. [▶a]

3 Join the rows together by crushing a crimp bead at each end of the necklace and securing the crimps inside the bead tips with a little glue. Attach the bead tips to the clasp (see page 10, step 3).

4 At various points on your necklace, knot 1.5m (58⅞in) strands of nylon thread on to your buttons. Attach the remaining buttons in different colours and sizes on to these strands as described in step 2, making sure they are evenly spaced. [▶b]

✱✱✱Whiter than white

A beautiful white design fit for a wedding day or other formal occasion.

Materials required

- White mother-of-pearl buttons, 16 x 22mm (⁷⁄₈in) in diameter, 16 x 18mm (¹¹⁄₁₆in) in diameter, 16 x 12mm (½in) in diameter
- 100 iridescent faceted beads, 4mm (⁵⁄₃₂in) in diameter
- 8.5m (9¼yd) fine stainless steel or brass wire
- 1.5m (58⁷⁄₈in) white muslin ribbon

1 Cut a 30cm (12in) length of wire. Thread on a small button. Double up the wire with the button at its centre and wind the button around on itself three times to twist the wire. [▶a]

2 Thread a faceted bead on to the twisted wires, then divide the wire to go through a medium-sized button, crossing the wires in the holes. Twist the wires and thread on a bead and then thread on a large button. Twist the end of the wire three times. Trim the excess wire. [▶b]

3 Repeat this process to create 16 identical motifs.

4 Cut six 60cm (23½in) lengths of wire which you will use to link the 16 motifs together. Work the wires in pairs over three parallel rows:
  – one row links the medium-sized buttons by their upper holes;
  – one row links the medium-sized buttons by their lower holes;
  – one row links the large buttons by their upper holes.
  Cross your wires in the button holes, twist them together twice and thread on a faceted bead. Then move on to the next motif. [▶c]

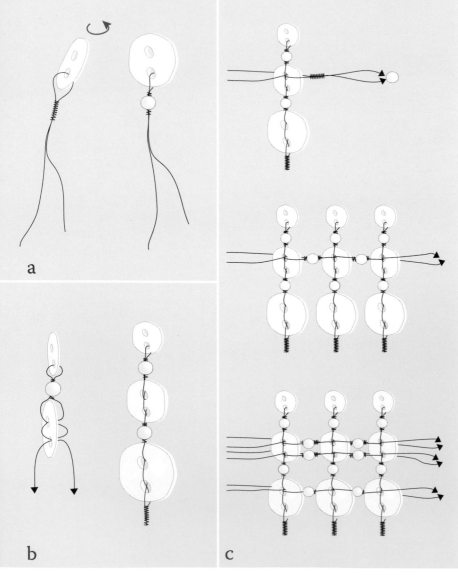

a

b

c

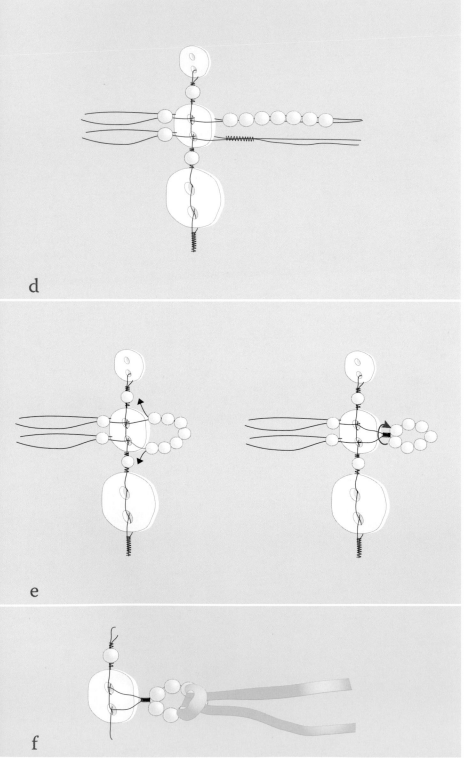

5 To finish, twist the ends of wire that link the top hole of the medium-sized buttons and thread seven faceted beads on to them. [▶**d**]

Twist the ends of wire from the bottom hole and then thread them into the same beads in the opposite direction to form a loop. Wind the excess wire between the beads and buttons. [▶**e**]

6 Do exactly the same at the other end creating a second loop. Cut the ribbon in half and attach to the loops. [▶**f**]

7 Finish off the wires linking the large buttons by twisting them together and bending them behind the buttons, securing with a little glue. Glue a bead at the base of each motif at the end of the twisted wire.

d

e

f

Hairpins

Simple hairpin

1 Thread a bead into the centre of the wire, fold in half and thread the two ends into the holes in your buttons, from the smallest to the largest. [▶a]

2 Gently twist the wire beneath the buttons. Wind the two wires around the top of the hairpin and back around the twisted wires. Trim the excess and apply a little glue. [▶b]

Button and bead hairpin

1 Thread a bead or button into the centre of the wire and twist it for about 2cm (¾in). [▶c]

2 Wind each of the two wires two or three times around the hairpin. Thread another bead or button on to one of the wires, about 3cm (1⅛in) from the hairpin and turn it around to twist the wire. Repeat this process, using both wires, to make up five or six strands of different lengths.

3 Finish each wire with two or three turns around the hairpin. Trim the excess wire and apply a little glue. Use round-nosed pliers to bend some of the wires in different directions.

Materials required
- 1 hairpin

Simple hairpin:
- 3 white or bronze mother-of-pearl buttons in various sizes
- 1 faceted bead or pearl bead
- 30cm (12in) stainless steel or brass wire

Button and bead hairpin:
- Assorted white and bronze buttons and beads in different sizes
- 1m (39¼in) stainless steel or brass wire

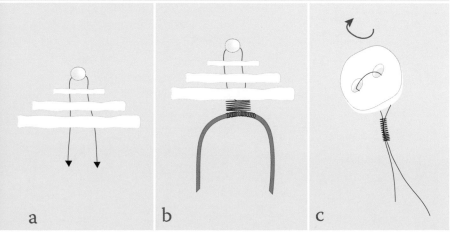

a   b   c

✷ Fit for a princess

These satin and pearl designs would make
a precious gift for a young girl.

Materials required: necklace

- 6–7 small natural mother-of-pearl two-hole buttons
  in a variety of shapes
- 60cm (23½in) very narrow satin ribbon

Materials required: rosette

- 3 buttons in different sizes, colours and/or shapes
  (they will be placed one on top of the other)
- 50cm (20in) coloured satin ribbon, about 1cm (³/₈in) wide
- 50cm (20in) ecru satin ribbon, about 5mm (³/₁₆in) wide
- 1 small brooch mount
- 1 small coloured faceted bead
- Needle and thread

a

Materials required: hairclip

- Natural mother-of-pearl buttons in various shapes and colours
- Small faceted beads
- Children's hairclips
- 20cm (8in) narrow satin ribbon per clip
- Fine stainless steel wire

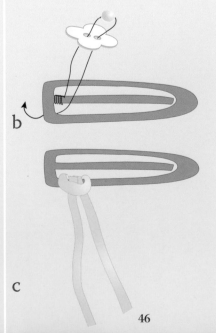

b

c

Necklace

Using a crewel needle or a doubled up length of metal wire, thread the ribbon through the buttons, alternating the shapes as you go. Leave ends to tie the necklace directly around your neck. A shorter length tied around your wrist will make a pretty bracelet.

Rosette

1 Lay the two ribbons one on top of the other and sew the three buttons with the small bead on top two thirds along the length of ribbon. [▶a]

2 Adjust the ribbons so they both hang down from the bottom of the motif and sew the brooch mount on to the back of the buttons. Cut the ends of the ribbons on the diagonal keeping them at different lengths.

Hairclip

Wind one end of the wire round the end of the clip and then thread it through the button and bead and secure it by winding it several times between the button and the clip before winding it round the clip. Trim the excess. [▶b]

As a variation, tie a length of ribbon to the clip and thread on a couple of buttons. [▶c]

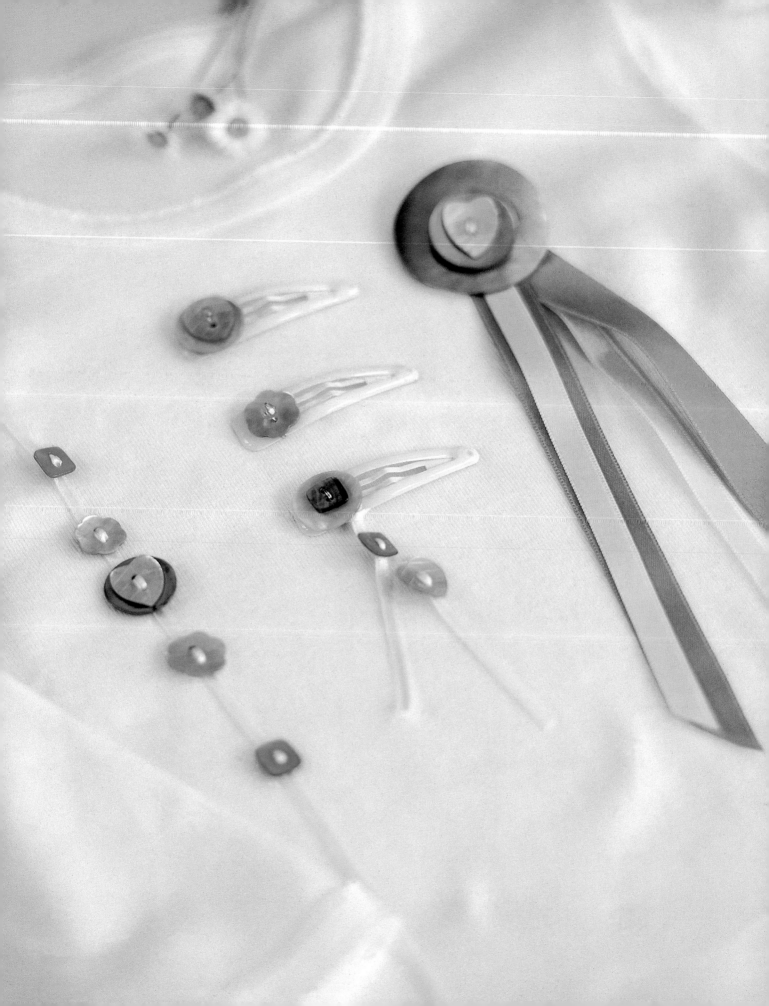

* Fireworks

This bright pendant will put a sparkle into any party.

Materials required: pendant
- 3–4 two-hole buttons in different colours and sizes
- 6m (6½yd) coloured elasticated nylon

a

b

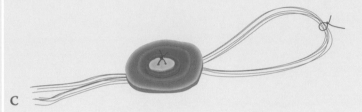
c

Materials required: bracelet
- Coloured two-hole buttons (3 or 5 depending on their size)
- Coloured elasticated nylon, 6 x 1.20m (47in) and 4 x 15cm (5⁶⁄₈in) per button
- 2 leather crimps
- 1 clasp
- 2 jump rings

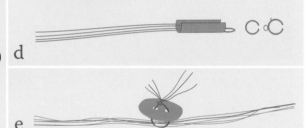
d

e

Pendant

1 Cut 6 x 80cm (31³⁄₈in) lengths of elasticated nylon and secure them at the centre by knotting a small strand of nylon around them. [▶a]

2 Place three or four buttons of different sizes and colours on top of each other. Thread 3 x 15cm (5⁶⁄₈in) nylon strands into these three buttons from the front to the back, round the 12 lengths forming the necklace and then back through the holes to the front. [▶b]

3 Tie a double knot in the ends of the threads on top of the buttons. Trim any excess threads to your desired length. [▶c]

4 Slide the buttons down the necklace to put it over your head and reposition them once in place.

Bracelet

1 Cut 6 x 20cm (8in) lengths of nylon.
Place one end of the six strands in a leather crimp with a little glue and gently crush the crimp. Decide on the length of your bracelet and trim before fitting the other crimp. Attach a clasp, using jump rings if necessary. [▶d]

2 Use four strands of nylon to attach your buttons tying them on in the same way as for the pendant and spacing them out at 1.5cm–3cm (⁵⁄₈–1⅛in) intervals depending on their size. Trim the excess nylon if necessary. [▶e]

✳✳ Child's play

These simple yet effective scoubidou designs will take you back to your childhood.

Materials required

- Shank buttons in fun shapes
- Scoubidou strands,
  2 to make the necklace, 1 for a bracelet
- Thick brass wire to slot into the scoubidou strands,
  1m (39¼in) for the necklace, 50cm (20in) for the bracelet

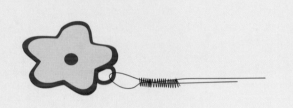

a

b

Use the same technique to make the necklace and the bracelet

1 Cut the scoubidou strands into 2–5cm (¾–2in) lengths.

2 Attach a button to the end of the brass wire and twist to form one half of the clasp. [▶a]

3 Thread a length of scoubidou on to the brass wire, then a button, and repeat this process, bending and twisting the wire as you work to create a wavy shape.

4 When you reach the desired length, make a button loop in the wire to fit over the clasp button. Twist the wire over itself, trim and crush to fix. [▶b]

hints and tips

Beware! The more you twist your brass wire, the shorter it will become. Make sure you bend it as you go along.

✳✳✳ Retro

Chic fabric-covered buttons make classy costume pieces in these matching designs.

Materials required

- About 15 button blanks in different sizes with pieces of fabric or assorted fabric-covered buttons
- 90cm (35¼in) medium-thick metal wire
- 2m (2⅛yd) narrow satin ribbon to match your buttons

1 Cover your buttons in the fabric of your choice. Referring to the instructions given with the button covering kits, place the fabric on top of the rounded button front and insert into the holder. Tuck in the fabric as carefully as you can and cover with the button back. Press down hard and take out your covered button. You can also use existing covered buttons. [▶a]

2 Fold the wire in half and twist it to make a small loop at the centre. Working on the reverse side of the buttons, thread each wire into a button shank, going through again to secure the button. [▶b]

3 Bring the two wires together and twist them around each other, then split them and thread each one through another pair of buttons. [▶c]

4 Repeat this process, positioning your buttons according to size, with the largest towards the centre. Keep the buttons tight together so the wires cannot be seen. [▶d]

5 Finish by making a small loop similar to the one you made at the start of your work. Cut the ribbon in half and attach each half to the loops. [▶e]

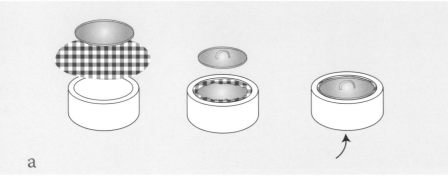

a

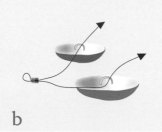

b

c

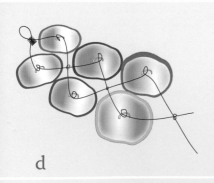

d

e

Hairslide and bracelet

Materials required: hairslide

- 6–8 assorted button blanks and fabric pieces or fabric-covered buttons
- 1 hairslide mount
- 60cm (23½in) thick metal wire

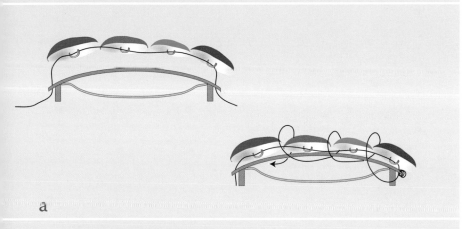

a

Materials required: bracelet

- 15–20 assorted fabric-covered buttons or button blanks in different sizes
- 1m (39¼in) medium-thick metal wire

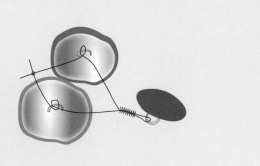

b

Hairslide

1 Prepare your buttons (see page 52, step 1) or use ready-covered fabric buttons.

2 Assemble your buttons in the same way as for the necklace to create a design that is the same size as the hairslide. Leaving an end of about 6cm (2⅜in) of wire, join the buttons with the wire as for the necklace.

3 Attach the design at each end to the holes in the hairslide mount by wrapping the wire around. Then wind the long end back along the upper part of the hairslide between the buttons and over your starting wire. Trim the excess and hide the end under a button. [▶a]

Bracelet

1 Make up your buttons (see page 52, step 1) or use ready-covered fabric buttons.

2 Fold the wire in half and twist to make a button loop at the centre that will fit over the button that you will use for the clasp.

3 Thread on the buttons, working on the reverse of the buttons in the same way as for the necklace.

4 Finish by threading the two wires into the clasp button. Twist the wires underneath it. Trim the excess wire and apply a little glue. [▶b]

✳✳ Porcupine

A delicate and original design punctuated with sparkling buttons.

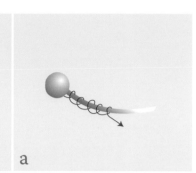

a

Materials required

- Assorted buttons and beads in different shades of a few colours
- 1 choker, 1 hairslide mount, 1 mesh ring mount
- Coloured copper wire: 8m (8¾yd) for the necklace, 3m (3¼yd) for the hairslide, 2m (2⅛yd) for the ring

b

c

d

Necklace

1 Cut the wire into two or three pieces to make it easier to work with. Start at one end of the choker and wind the copper wire around it quite tightly over about a quarter of the length of the necklace. [▶a]

2 Thread on a button 3cm (1⅛in) away from the choker, bend the wire back and turn the button around on itself to twist the wire. Repeat this process, using buttons and beads, winding the wire three or four times around the choker between each 'quill'. [▶b]

3 Stop adding quills for the last quarter of the choker and finish by winding the wire as in step 1. Apply a little glue to the ends to secure.

Hairslide

Secure the wire to the hole at the end of the hairslide. Work in the same way as for the necklace, winding the wire around the upper part of the slide and adding quills of beads. Secure the wire in the hole at the other end. [▶c]

Ring

1 Thread the wire into a hole in the mesh. Thread on a button 2cm (¾in) from the mesh, bend the wire back and go back into a hole in the mesh. Turn the button around on itself to twist the wire. [▶d]

2 Bring the wire out at another point and repeat the process until your ring mount is covered. Secure the ends of the wire under the mesh by twisting them and applying a little glue. Assemble the ring by pulling the claws down over the mesh.

✳✳ Button frenzy

These brightly coloured buttons on metallic threads make superbly funky pieces.

Materials required
- Assorted two-hole buttons
- 3m (3¼yd) coloured tiger tail in various colours
- 20 crimp beads
- 2 bead tips and 2 jump rings
- 1 clasp

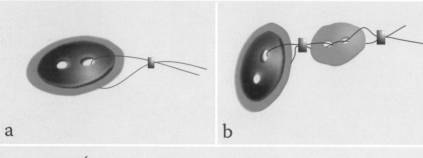

a

b

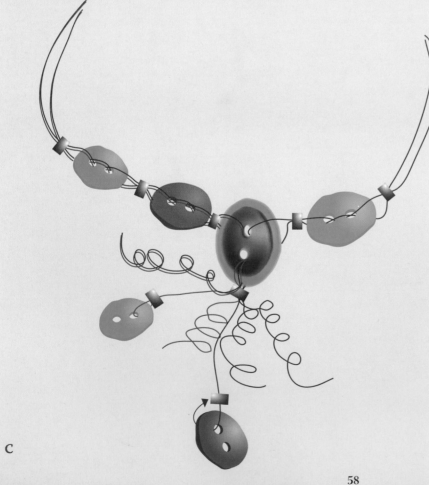

c

1 Cut 2 x 50cm (20in) lengths of tiger tail. Secure one to the central buttons (two buttons have been used here but you may use one if you wish) by threading on a crimp bead, the central buttons, and back through the crimp bead. Position the buttons at the centre of the tiger tail before crushing the crimp as close to the button as possible with flat-nosed pliers. [▶a]

2 Attach another button adjacent to the central button, crossing the tiger tail in the holes, and secure with a crimp bead. [▶b]
   Add two smaller buttons on the other side in the same way using a second length of tiger tail.

3 Cut 3 x 30cm (12in) lengths of tiger tail and thread them through the second hole in the central buttons. If possible, secure these six strands in the same crimp bead below the button.

4 Use scissors to curl some of the lengths by running the strand between the blade and your thumb. Attach buttons to the other lengths using crimp beads. Trim any excess tiger tail. [▶c]

5 Decide how long you want your necklace. Trim and thread on crimp beads at the ends of the tiger tail, crush and then secure the crimps in bead tips with a little glue. Attach the clasp, using jump rings if necessary (see page 10, step 3).

Bracelet, rings and earrings

Materials required: bracelet

- 5–6 assorted two-hole buttons
- 6 x 20cm (8in) tiger tail in two or three colours
- 12-14 crimp beads
- 2 bead tips
- 1 clasp

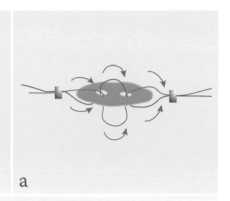

a

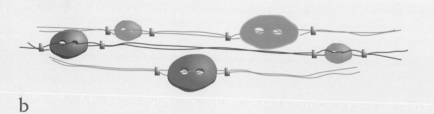

b

Materials required: rings

- 1 or 2 buttons per ring
- 75cm (29½in) tiger tail
- 1 mesh ring mount
- 3 crimp beads

Materials required: earrings

- 2 buttons per earring
- 30cm (12in) coloured tiger tail
- 2 fishhook earwires

Bracelet

Make up the three rows at the same time to ensure your buttons are evenly spaced

1 Take 6 x 20cm (8in) lengths of tiger tail and secure them together at one end with a crimp bead. Using two strands thread on a crimp bead and then the first button, crossing the tiger tail in the holes of the button, then secure the button by crushing the crimp beads, keeping the wire taut. [▶a]

2 Repeat this process over the three rows, spacing your buttons out so that your bracelet looks balanced. [▶b]
  Check the length of the bracelet, trim and secure the other ends together with a crimp bead.

3 Use bead tips to attach the clasp to the crimps (see page 10, step 3).

Rings

1 Cut the tiger tail into three sections. Thread the strands through a hole in the button, then through the mesh and back up through the second hole in the button.

2 Crush a crimp on the tiger tail to secure. Curl the tiger tail as described on page 58, step 4.

3 Fit the mesh to the mount by pulling down the claws. As a variation thread small buttons or beads on to the tiger tail before securing with crimps.

Earrings

1 Fold a 15cm (5⁶/₈in) length of tiger tail in half and thread it into the earwire loop and secure with a crimp bead.

2 Thread on your first button, crossing the tiger tail through the button, then crush a crimp bead below it. Repeat the process with the other buttons.

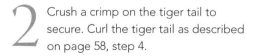

hints and tips

Why not attach several buttons to the same ring? Brighten up all these designs by using a variety of coloured tiger tail.

✳✳ Felt and buttons

Soft, warm materials add a personal touch to your winter wear.

Materials required: necklace

- 3 large buttons in natural mother-of-pearl, about 4cm (1½in) in diameter)
- 5 natural mother-of-pearl buttons, 1cm (³⁄₈in) in diameter, 3 for the design and 2 for assembly
- 25cm (9⁷⁄₈in) square of ecru felt
- 40cm (15⁵⁄₈in) square of charcoal grey felt
- Grey sewing thread and needle

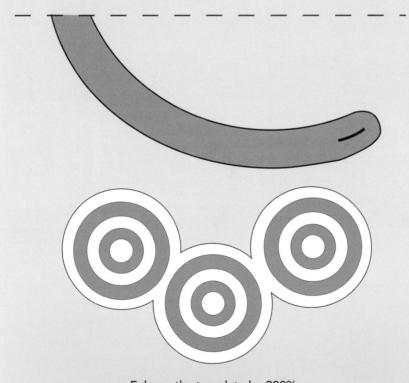

Enlarge the template by 200%.

Enlarge the template by 200%.

Necklace

1 Using the template provided, cut out the three-circle shape from ecru felt, which is the base for the necklace design. Cut out 3 x 5cm (2in) circles and 3 x 2.5cm (1in) circles from the charcoal grey felt. Lastly, cut out the strip that will go around your neck.

2 Lay a large charcoal grey circle, a large mother-of-pearl button, a small charcoal grey circle and a small mother-of-pearl button on each of the three circle motifs. Sew these on together through the button holes.

3 On the reverse of your work, sew the two remaining mother-of-pearl buttons on each side to attach the strip that will go around your neck. Use scissors to cut a buttonhole at each end of the strip.

Bracelet

1 Cut out the bracelet shape from charcoal grey felt, using the template as a guide. You may need to adjust the size to fit your wrist.

2 Cut a buttonhole at one end of the bracelet. Sew on the button that will act as the clasp at the other end. The remaining buttons are sewn on at random. Add a contrast circle of felt and another button on top of a few of the larger buttons, as on the necklace.

Acknowledgements

- Lune Rousse in Tours, France, which helped in the making of this publication.

- La Droguerie in Paris, which introduced the author to the joys of beads and buttons many years ago.

- Friends and colleagues, for their suggestions and their sound advice.

- Hélène and Edmond, for their support and encouragement.

Addresses

You'll find buttons and beads hidden away in drawers, old sewing boxes and even garage sales, but you can also get them – together with the basic equipment used in this book – from:

UK

Fred Aldous Ltd
37 Lever Street,
Manchester, M1 1LW
Tel. 0870 751 7301
www.fredaldous.co.uk

Gregory Knopp online
PO Box 158,
Gillingham, ME7 3HF
01634 357706
www.gregory.knopp.co.uk

Josy Rose Ltd.
PO Box 44204,
London, E3 EXB
0845 450 1212
www.josyrose.com

Regalcrafts
269 Meadow Way,
Leighton Buzzard, LU7 3XS
www.regalcrafts.com

The Rocking Rabbit Trading Co
7 The Green,
Haddenham, CB6 3TA
Tel. 0870 606 1588
www.rockingrabbit.co.uk

USA

As Cute as a Button
Canon St Ste G,
San Diego, CA 92106, USA
Tel. 619 223 2555
www.ascuteasabutton.com

Brightlings Beads
107 Milley Brook Court,
Cary, NC 27519, USA
Tel. 919 388 9822
www.brightlingsbeads.com

Crafts 4 Me
PO Box 1716,
Discovery Bay, CA 94514
1 800 917 7888
www.crafts4me.com

Shelly's Buttons and More
308 Yacht Club Drive,
Berlin, MD 21811
888 811 7441
www.dressitupbuttonsandtrim.com